2021 EDITION
My Girly Unicorn
Amigurumi Crochet Doll Pattern

Colors, Quantity and Type

There are 8 different colors used to make My Girly
Unicorn Amiguumi Crochet Doll. The main color is a light pink
which is used to make the head, body, arms, and legs.
The YarnArt Jeans color is Pink Blush No. 18.
Quantity Needed: approximately 200-250 yards.

The secondary color is a medium pink used to represent the
hooves. The YarnArt Jeans color is Antique Rose No. 80.
Quantity needed: approximately 80 yards.

The other YarnArt Jeans colors used to make the hair, tail, bangs,
and horn are as follows: Lemon No. 67, Mint Green No. 79,
Spring Green No. 29, Light Peach No. 73, Lovely Lilac No. 19,
Powder Blue No. 75.
Quantity needed: approximately 10 yards.

Yard Type: YarnArt Jeans #1 super fine, 4-ply.

TOOLS AND MATERIALS USED:
Yarn art Jeans
Eyes 8mm
2.2 - 2.5mm hook

STITCH SYMBOL:

Ch	Chain	
X	Single crochet	
V	Increase (make 2X in one st)	
A	Decrease (make a X in two st)	
W	3 single crochets in the same st (Make 3X in one st)	
M	1 single crochets 3 stitches together	
T	Half Double crochet	
TV	Half Double crochet increase (make 2T in one st)	
TA	Half Double crochet decrease (make a T in two st)	
F	Double crochet	
FV	FV Double crochet increase (make 2F in one st)	
FA	Double crochet decrease (make a F in two st)	
FW	3 double crochet in the same stitch (Make 3F in one st)	
FM	1 Double crochet 3 stitches together	
SLST	Slip stitch	
SK	skip	
BLO	BLO Back loops only	
FLO	Front Loops only	
...	Repeat	
MR	Magic ring	

Slowly Stuff As You Go

Brand: We recommend Morning Glory Cluster because it doesn't need to be pulled apart and is quite fluffy out of the package. It is reasonably-priced and can be purchased at Wal-Mart.

Test: After you have made a body part, test your crochet by adding a handful of stuffing. If you see the stuffing through the stitches, you need to make a change. One solution: drop down in hook size. If the stuffing is too tightly packed, squeeze outside with hands to loosen it.

Head: When you have made a few rounds of crochet decreases, add a large handful of stuffing **(Insert eyes into head between Round 16 and 17, See Instructions on Page 7).** Be careful not to add too much stuffing because you will find it difficult to decrease smoothly. When you arrive at the last 12 stitches in a round, stop decreasing and add stuffing. Be sure to push stuffing to the sides first in order to firm up the outer edges. Use hands on the outside of head to shape the head, as if molding clay. When you decrease to 6 stitches, continue stuffing until head is full. Continue to last round, adding stuffing as needed.

Neck: Structurally, this is the most important part. Keep the neck short and wide. Stuff it tightly and extra firm because it will be supporting a heavy head with a lot of curls. If the neck is weak, the head will droop forward, backward, or both. Use the end of your crochet hook to help add extra stuffing.

Slowly Stuff As You Go (cont.)

Body: Place a large handful of stuffing inside the body cavity **before** starting your crochet decreases. If it is too full, you will encounter resistance as you crochet. Remove some stuffing until resistance is no longer encountered. If you attempt to ignore resistance and continue to crochet, you may end up with holes or spaces in your decreases. As you add stuffing inside the body, push it to the sides to make certain the edges are filled. This will prevent gaps.

Arms, Legs, and Horn: Stuffing is based on your preference for these body parts. They are not essential to the support structure of the doll. But, in any case, make sure the stuffing is firm. Use your crochet hook to push stuffing into the edges.

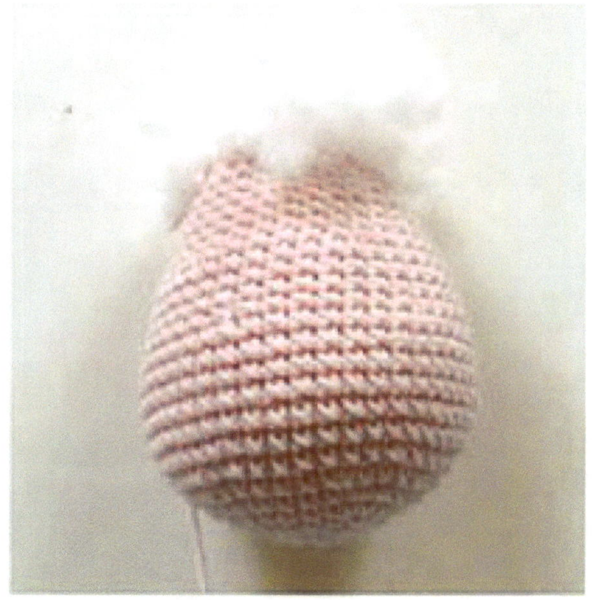

Body

HEAD

ROUND 1: 6 single crochet in a magic ring
ROUND 2: 1 increase in each stitch of previous round (12)
ROUND 3: (1 single crochet, 1 increase) repeat 6 times (18)
ROUND 4: (2 single crochet, 1 increase) repeat 6 times (24)
ROUND 5: (3 single crochet, 1 increase) repeat 6 times (30)
ROUND 6: (4 single crochet, 1 increase) repeat 6 times (36)
ROUND 7/8/9/10/11/12/13: 1 single crochet in each stitch of previous round (36)
ROUND 14: (6 single crochet, 1 increase) repeat 3 times, and continue with a single crochet until the end of the round. (39)
ROUND 15: (7 single crochet, 1 increase) repeat 3 times, and continue with a single crochet until the end of the round. (42)
ROUND 16: (8 single crochet, 1 increase) repeat 3 times, and continue with a single crochet until the end of the round **(Insert eyes into head. See instructions on Page 7)** (45)
ROUND 17: (9 single crochet, 1 increase) repeat 3 times, and continue with a single crochet until the end of the round (48)
ROUND 18/19/20/21/22/23/24/25: 1 single crochet in each stitch of previous round (48)
ROUND 26: (6 single crochet, 1 decrease) repeat 6 times (42)
ROUND 27: (5 single crochet, 1 decrease) repeat 6 times (36)
ROUND 28: (4 single crochet, 1 decrease) repeat 6 times (30)
ROUND 29: (3 single crochet, 1 decrease) repeat 6 times (24)
ROUND 30: (2 single crochet, 1 decrease) repeat 6 times (18)
ROUND 31: (1 single crochet, 1 decrease) repeat 6 times (12)
ROUND 32: 6 decrease (6)

How To Install The Eyes

Note: The doll made from the instructions in this pattern is for children age 4 and up. Plastic eyes can become a choking hazard for children under age 4. Always use under adult supervision.

Procedure: In Figure 1 below is a picture of the plastic eyes. To install the eyes, stick the pointed end into the head between Round 16 and 17 (See figure 3 and 4 below), **before adding stuffing.** From the inside, move the washer (See Figure 1) over the tip and up to the eye (See Figure 2). At this point, from the inside, you move the washer forward and it will make a "click" sound when it is in place.

Figure 1   Figure 2   Figure 3   Figure 4

BODY:

ROUND 1: 6 single crochet in a magic ring
ROUND 2: 1 increase in each stitch of previous round (12)
ROUND 3: (1 single crochet, 1 increase) repeat 6 times (18)
ROUND 4: (2 single crochet, 1 increase) repeat 6 times (24)
ROUND 5: (3 single crochet, 1 increase) repeat 6 times (30)
ROUND 6: (4 single crochet, 1 increase) repeat 6 rimes (36)
ROUND 7: (5 single crochet, 1 increase) repeat 6 times (42)
ROUND 8: (6 single crochet, 1 increase) repeat 6 times (48)
ROUND 9/10/11/12/13/14: 1 single crochet in each stitch of previous round (48)
ROUND 15: (6 single crochet, 1 decrease) repeat 6 times (42)
ROUND 16-18: 1 single crochet in each stitch of previous round (42)
ROUND 19: (5 single crochet, 1 decrease) repeat 6 times (36)
ROUND 20-22 1 single crochet in each stitch of previous round (36)
ROUND 23: (4 single crochet, 1 decrease) repeat 6 times (30)
ROUND 24-25: 1 single crochet in each stitch of previous round (30)
ROUND 26: (3 single crochet, 1 decrease) repeat 6 times (24)
ROUND 27-28: 1 single crochet in eachs titch of previous round (24)
ROUND 29: (2 single crochet, 1 decrease) repeat 6 times (18)
ROUND 30: 1 single crochet in each stitch of previous round (18)
ROUND 31: (2 single crochet, 1 increase) repeat 6 times (24)
ROUND 32: (3 single crochet, 1 increase) repeat 6 times (30)

End off, leave tail for sewing

ARMS:

begin with pink yarn

ROUND 1: 6 single crochet in a magic ring

ROUND 2: 1 increase in each stitch of previous round (12)

ROUND 3: (1 single crochet, 1 increase) repeat 6 times (18)

ROUND 4: (2 single crochet, 1 increase) repeat 6 times (24)

ROUND 5-8: 1 single crochet in each stitch of previous round (24)

ROUND 9: (2 single crochet, 1 decrease) repeat 6 times (18)

ROUND 10: 1 single crochet in each stitch of previous round (18)

change to light pink yarn

ROUND 11-13: 1 single crochet in each stitch of previous round (18)

ROUND 14: (4 single crochet, 1 decrease) repeat 3 times (15)

ROUND 15: 1 single crochet in each stitch of previous round (15)

ROUND 16: (3 single crochet, 1 decrease) repeat 3 times (12)

ROUND 17-29: 1 single crochet in each stitch of previous round (12)

ROUND 30: 6 decrease

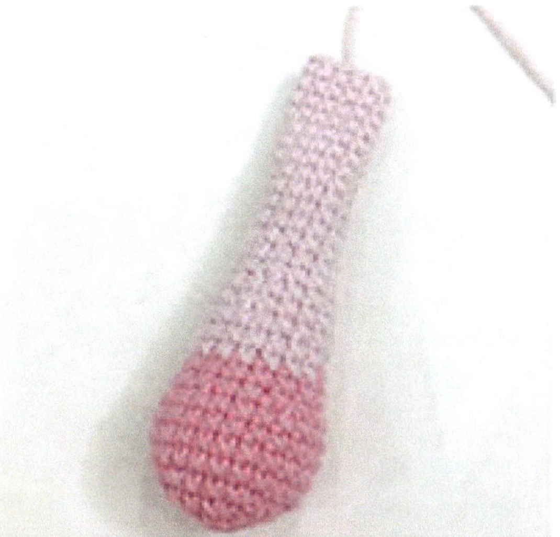

LEGS:
begin with pink yarn

ROUND 1: 6 single crochet in a magic ring
ROUND 2: 1 increase in each stitch of previous round (12)
ROUND 3: (1 single crochet, 1 increase) repeat 6 times (18)
ROUND 4: (2 single crochet, 1 increase) repeat 6 times (24)
ROUND 5: (3 single crochet, 1 increase) repeat 6 times (30)
ROUND 6-11: 1 single crochet in each stitch of previous round (30)
ROUND 12: 9 single crochet, 1 decrease, 3 single crochet, 1 decrease, 3 single crochet, 1 decrease, 9 single crochet (27)
ROUND 13: 8 single crochet, 1 decrease, 3 single crochet, 1 decrease, 3 single crochet, 1 decrease, 7 single crochet (24)

change to light pink yarn

ROUND 14-16: 1 single crochet in each stitch of previous round (24)
ROUND 17: (6 single crochet, 1 decrease) repeat 3 times (21)
ROUND 18-19: 1 single crochet in each stitch of previous round (21)
ROUND 20: (5 single crochet, 1 decrease) repeat 3 times (18)
ROUND 21-22: 1 single crochet in each stitch of previous round (18)
ROUND 23: (4 single crochet, 1 decrease) repeat 3 times (15)
ROUND 24-28: 1 single crochet in each stitch of previous round (15)

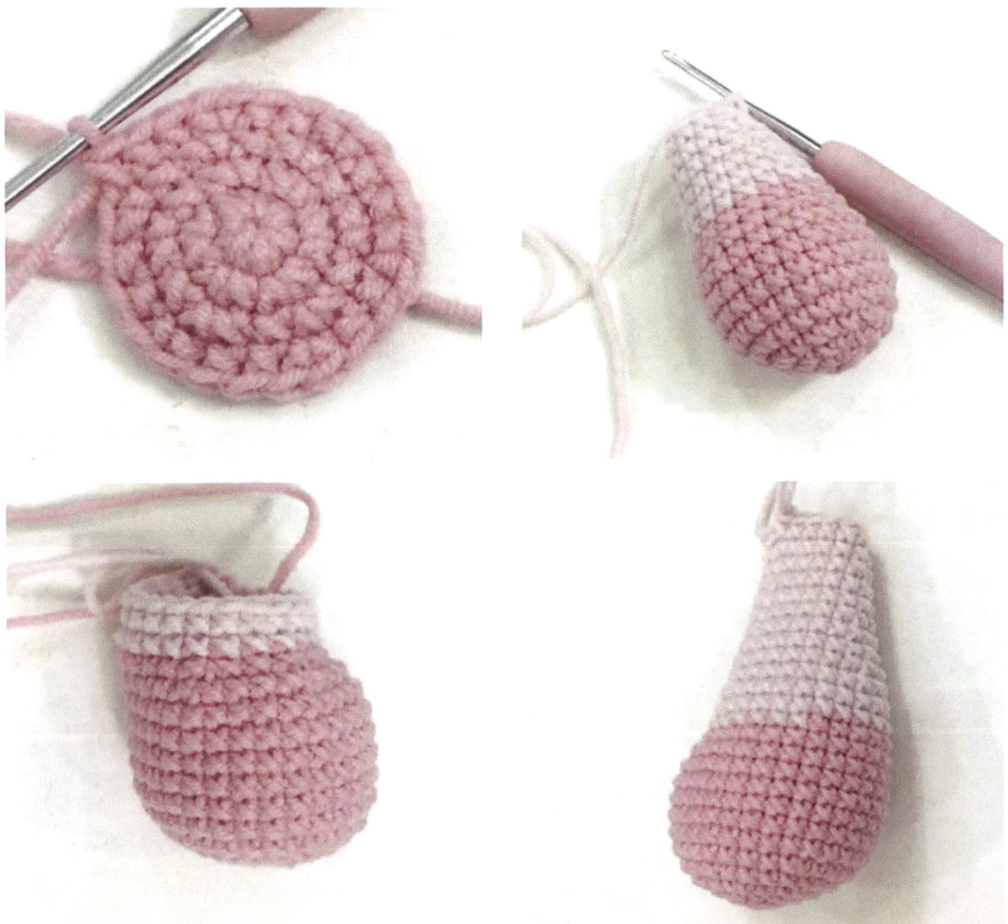

EARS:
part1:
ROUND 1: 5 single crochet in a magic ring (5)
ROUND 2: 1 single crochet in each stitch of previous round (5)
ROUND 3: 1 increase in each stitch of previous round (10)
ROUND 4: 1 single crochet in each stitch of previous round (10)
ROUND 5: (1 single crochet, 1 increase) repeat 5 times (15)
ROUND 6-8/9: 1 single crochet in each stitch of previous round (15)

part2:
ROUND 1: 7 chain, 1 single crochet in second chain from hook, 4 single crochet, 3 single crochets in the same st , 5 single crochet

sew part 1 with part 2

HORN

ROUND 1: 5 single crochet in a magic ring (5)
ROUND 2: 1 single crochet in each stitch of previous round (5)
ROUND 3: 1 increase in each stitch of previous round (10)
ROUND 4: 1 single crochet in each stitch of previous round (10)
ROUND 5: (1 single crochet, 1 increase) repeat 5 times (15)
ROUND 6-8/9: 1 single crochet in each stitch of previous round (15)

End off, leave tail

HAIR: 24 couple strands

H1: 61 chain, 1 single crochet in second chain from hook, 59 single crochet, continue, 61 chain, 1 single crochet in second chain from hook, 59 single crochet.

To view our video on how to make the curls, please go to our youtube video located at https://youtu.be/acpgBzPLVlM

How To Get The Curls

1.) We use the Single Crochet Curley Cue method.

2.) Start one-third of the way from the end of one side of the chain. At this point, start doing 3 single crochets into each stitch. Gradually, little spirals will start to form.

3.) Continue the procedure in Step 2. Keep doing 3 single crochets into each stitch until you reach the end of the chain.

4.) After you have reached the end of the chain, rework the spirals with your hands, twisting the spiral tighter. You are finished.

For the tail, you would use the same procedure, except you would use a crochet chain 3.5 inches long and start Step 2 at one end and do 3 single crochets into each stitch until you come to the end of the chain. The entire chain would be spiral curls.

The Bangs

Yarn needed: Six (6) 1.25 inch strips from single stitch crochet chain. You can use leftovers from doing the hair in the back.

Procedure: The bangs are stitched around the horn, at the base, in a semi-circle from the middle of the left side of the horn, across the front, and ending at the middle of the right side of the horn.

Looking at the face of the doll and going from left to right, the first strip is YarnArt Jeans color Lemon No. 67. It is attached to the left side of the horn. The second strip is YarnArt Jeans color Mint Green No. 79. It is attached in front of the Lemon strip, circling around the horn. The third strip is YarnArt Jeans color Light Peach No. 73. It is attached in front of the Mint Green strip. The fourth strip is YarnArt Jeans color Lovely Lilac No. 19. it is attached in front of the Light Peach strip. The fifth strip is YarnArt Jeans color Powder Blue No. 75. It is attached in front of the Lovely Lilac strip. The sixth and final strip is YarnArt Jeans color Antique Rose No. 80. It is attached in front of the Powder Blue strip. At this point, you should have the Antique Rose strip on the opposite side ofthe horn from the Lemon strip. You are finished.

ASSEMBLED INSTRUCTIONS
head and body

ASSEMBLED INSTRUCTIONS

Horn and head

ASSEMBLED INSTRUCTIONS

Hair and head

ASSEMBLED INSTRUCTIONS

Hair and head

ASSEMBLED INSTRUCTIONS

Ears and head
sew the ears on the head between rows 25 and 26

ASSEMBLED INSTRUCTIONS

ARMS AND FOOTS

Tail: 8 strands
H1: 31 chain, 1 single crochet in second chain from hook, 29 single crochet.
Sew the tails on the body between rows 9 and 10

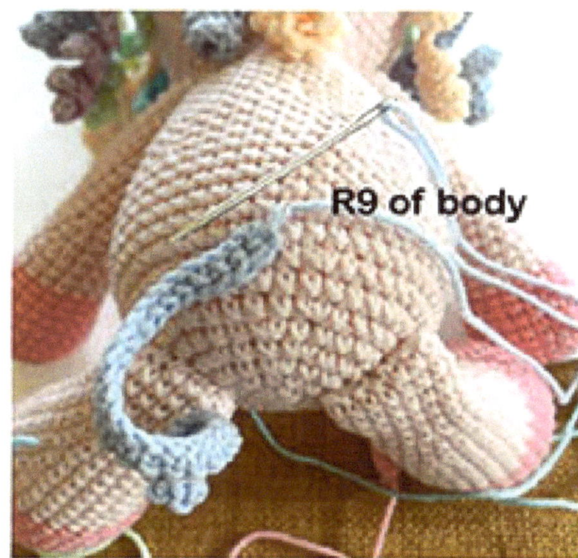

ASSEMBLED INSTRUCTIONS

eyelashes

www.ingramcontent.com/pod-product-compliance
Lightning Source LLC
Chambersburg PA
CBHW042124110726
48006CB00003B/754